AI

OBEY THE VOICE OF GOD

Jolyn Richards

Jolyn

Revelation 2:7 He who has an ear, let him hear what the Spirit says to the churches. To him who overcomes, I will grant to eat of the tree of life which is in the Paradise of God.

Tree of Life Bible Studies, L.L.C.
Maquoketa, Iowa 52060
tolbiblestudies@gmail.com
www.treeoflifebiblestudies.com

ANGELS
Obey the Voice of God

Tree of Life Bible Studies, L.L.C.
18040 110th St
Maquoketa, Iowa 52060 USA
e-mail: tolbiblestudies@gmail.com
Website: www.treeoflifebiblestudies.com

ISBN: 978-0-9894954-3-1

Copyright © 2009, 2011 Jolyn Richards

Photo Copyright © 2009 Jolyn Richards

Printed in the United States of America

Dedication
To my only daughter Karysa Jolyn Richards

We have three sons and the thought of having a daughter seemed like it might not be God's plan. My husband is the youngest of four boys and I thought that our next baby would also be a boy. I read about different ways to help you have a girl, but prayed for God's will to be done for our family. Karysa was born October 17, 1999 on a Sunday afternoon. Her nursery was decorated with angels and painted lavender. She is truly our "angel baby" gift from God and I love being her mom. I pray that as she grows she will follow God and the angels will watch over her.

Author's Note

I felt God leading me to write about angels. I was unsure if this was what He really wanted me to write about, so I asked people in my classes to pray for me. God can use people for what He wants done. I started receiving newspaper clippings, books, cards, and photos. I even heard stories and received a music tape all with things about angels.

Jane ordered me a magazine subscription, *Angels on Earth*, from Guideposts about angels. Lucinda gave my 9 year old daughter Karysa, a box of 80 angel stickers that she was delighted about. Her instructions were to put them all over the house so I would find them and be reminded to write about angels. I see angels everywhere and on all the light switch covers around our home. This was the encouragement that I needed to write. The best part is that just when I thought it seemed impossible, that is when someone would give me something or ask me how the study was going.

Thank you to all the people that obeyed God's voice and encouraged me while I wrote about angels. Thanks mom and David (my husband) for taking my classes, listening and supporting me. I have felt God's presence throughout this journey and believe that angels are around us even if we are unaware. People are not angels but they are out there watching and obeying the voice of God. We are to listen and obey God's voice like angels do.

Grace and peace,

Jolyn

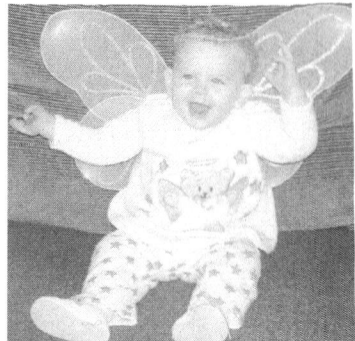

ANGELS
Obey the Voice of God

Introduction	Helping You With The Study Before You Begin............................	6
Lesson 1	Creation & Appearance	8
Lesson 2	Cherubim & Ark of the Covenant	13
Lesson 3	Cherubim with Wheels	20
Lesson 4	Seraphim	27
Lesson 5	Angel Gabriel to Zacharias & Mary	33
Lesson 6	Gabriel, Michael & Fallen Angels	42
Lesson 7	Jesus & Angels	50
Lesson 8	Amount of Angels & Purpose	59
Lesson 9	Angels Worship & Praise	65
Lesson 10	Angels with Messages	71
Lesson 11	Zechariah's Visions & Jesus' Return	79
Lesson 12	Angels of Revelation	85

HELPING YOU WITH THE STUDY

<u>Share and care:</u> Get to know others using short answers. Break into smaller groups if over 20 in a class.

<u>Prayer:</u> Let the Holy Spirit guide you.

<u>Read Scripture:</u> Take turns reading aloud or pass. I like using the New American Standard Bible.

<u>Answer Questions:</u> Find facts using Scripture so you learn the Word. Let those who want to participate shout out and have a leader write answers down on a board.

<u>Charts & Maps:</u> Look for references to share. I recommend using *Rose Book of Bible Charts, Maps and Timelines from Rose Publishing* since you are able to reproduce for your class. Order one from our website.

<u>Focus on the Facts:</u> Summary of what you learned.

<u>So What?</u> How does what I learned apply to my life? Share and encourage each other.

<u>Lord's Prayer:</u> Say together (Matt 6:9-13) or any prayer.

<u>About Angels:</u> At the end of each lesson you will have a fact about angels that you can share. Each week use page 94 to review what you have learned.

<u>1 Peter 4:7-11</u> **The end of all things is near; therefore, be of sound judgment and sober spirit for the purpose of prayer. Above all, keep fervent in your love for one another, because love covers a multitude of sins. Be hospitable to one another without complaint. As each one has received a special gift, employ it in serving one another as good stewards of the manifold grace of God. Whoever speaks, is to do so as one who is speaking the utterances of God; whoever serves is to do so as one who is serving by the strength which God supplies; so that in all things God may be glorified through Jesus Christ, to whom belongs the glory and dominion forever and ever. Amen.**

BEFORE YOU BEGIN

Angels are divine messengers from God. They worship, obey and praise Him. The Bible gives us details about angels in about 300 Scriptures (although I have not used them all) so we will learn the truth about them.

It is Christmas time as I begin to write this study about angels. We see different images of what angels might look like. This leads me to wonder about what angels really do look like, who they are, where they are and what purpose they serve. I believe there are angels, although appearances are uncommon and will only happen to a few people.

It is important to understand that we are to worship God and not angels. They obey God and not man. Do not be deceived into believing in Satan and his fallen angels. Believe in God and Jesus! The cover title was inspired by **Psalm 103:20 Bless the LORD, you His angels, Mighty in strength, who perform His word, Obeying the voice of His word!**

An archangel will shout when Jesus returns and the angels of Revelation will sound their trumpets during the end times. **1 Thessalonians 4:16 For the Lord Himself will descend from heaven with a shout, with the voice of the archangel and with the trumpet of God and the dead in Christ will rise first.** The photo on the cover was taken in Elveden, England of the top of a church.

This study will take you all over the Bible. When I taught this class it was helpful to assign students different scripture for the lesson before class started so they were ready to read when their scripture came up. Not everyone will feel comfortable reading aloud so just ask those that want to. If you have a class of students that know their Bibles well or would like to learn them better they may like following along.

LESSON ONE
Creation & Appearance

Share and care: Share the first thing you think about angels.

Prayer

1. Read <u>John 1:1-3,14</u>.

    a. Who was in the beginning? (1:1-2,14)

    b. What came into being through Him? (1:3)

2. Read <u>Colossians 1:15-17</u>.

    a. What did you learn about Christ? (1:15)

    b. Write out what was created by Him and why? (1:16-17)

3. Using the information you have gained, who created angels?

4. Read <u>Matthew 28:1-4</u>.

    a. Where did the angel of the Lord come from? (28:2)

    b. What did the angel do? (28:2)

    c. What did the angel look like? (28:3)

    d. What happened to the guards after they saw him? (28:4)

5. Read <u>Luke 24:1-4, 22, 23</u>.

    a. Two men suddenly stood near. What did they look like? (24:4)

    b. Who were the two men? (24:23)

6. Read <u>2 Thessalonians 1:6-8</u>. How are the angels described? (1:7)

7. Read <u>Hebrews 1:7</u>. How are angels described?

8. **Daniel 9:21** (NKJV) Yes, while I was speaking in prayer, the man Gabriel, whom I had seen in the vision at the beginning, being caused to fly swiftly, reached me about the time of the evening offering.

   How did angel Gabriel come to Daniel?

9. **Read 2 Samuel 22:11. In the Song of David, how is the cherub described?**

10. **Read Genesis 18:1-8,22.**

    a. **Who appeared to Abraham? (18:1)**

    b. **Who did Abraham see? (18:2)**

    c. **What did the men eat? (18:6-8)**

    d. **Where did the two men go? Who stayed? (18:22)**

11. **Read Genesis 19:1-3.**

    a. **Who were the two men? (19:1)**

    b. **What did Lot serve the angels? (19:3)**

12. Read <u>Psalm 78:23-25</u>.

   a. Where did the manna come from? (78:23)

   b. What did man eat? (78:24-25)

13. Read <u>Hebrews 13:1-2</u>. Why should we show hospitality to strangers?

FOCUS ON THE FACTS

God and Jesus were in the beginning. All things were created in the heavens and earth, visible and invisible. Angels were created by God through Jesus for God. Even though the Scriptures do not specifically state when angels were created, we know that they were created! The angel seen at Jesus' tomb descended from heaven (after a severe earthquake), rolled away the stone and sat upon it. His appearance was like lightning and his clothing was white as snow. The guards were afraid and fell like dead men. The angels in Luke suddenly appeared and had dazzling clothing. Angels are also described as mighty in flaming fire or like wind. Some angels came in human form and others came flying swiftly. Two angels appeared to Abraham and Lot and they ate with them. In Psalms we found out that manna came from heaven, the bread of angels. We should show hospitality to strangers because we may be entertaining angels without knowing it.

SO WHAT?

The Trinity is God, Jesus and the Holy Spirit. The Word (Jesus) was with God in the beginning and Jesus became flesh as human, when born as a baby. We receive the Holy Spirit when we become believers.

Do you think that people can still see angels today? How would you feel if you encountered an angel? Do you think you would be afraid or excited? When angels are seen many times the people are told not to be afraid.

What are your thoughts about the different ways that angels are described? We will be learning about more ways that angels are described in the next few lessons. Angels can come in different ways to those who need them. They may even be a stranger that has come to lend a helping hand. Have you had an encounter with an angel or known someone that has? Please share if you feel comfortable.

Personally I have not seen an angel as far as I know. Don't worry if you have not seen one since sightings are more rare than common. As you learn more about angels you will be more aware of your surroundings and you never know when you might come across one.

I have read several stories about angels and they have touched my heart. Check your library or internet for short angel stories or articles to share with class. This is an interesting way to share what God does in other people's lives using angels. I recommend:

Angels: God's Secret Agents by Billy Graham
www.angelsonearth.com
Angels on Earth a magazine by Guideposts

ANGELS WERE CREATED FOR GOD

LORD'S PRAYER

LESSON TWO
Cherubim & Ark of the Covenant

Share and care: Where do you usually hear God talking
to you?

Prayer

Cherubim are celestial beings (angels) with wings that
guard. **Cherub** is singular.

1.   Read <u>Genesis 3:17-24</u>.

   a. What did Adam do in <u>Genesis 3:17</u>?

   b. What did Adam name his wife? (3:20)

   c. Who made garments of skin for them? (3:21)
      This is the first bloodshed.

   d. What did Adam and Eve now know? (3:22)

   e. What could happen to them? (3:22)

   f. Where did the LORD God send them? (3:23)

   g. Who was stationed at the east of the garden of
      Eden? Why? (3:24)

2. Read Exodus 25:1-22

a. Who did the LORD speak to? (25:1)

b. What did the sons of Israel construct? Why? (25:8)

c. What was put into the ark? (25:16)

d. What was on top of the ark? (25:17)

e. What was made for it? (25:18)

f. How were they placed? (25:19)

g. Ark of the Covenant (25:20-22)

3. Read <u>Hebrews 9:1-10</u>.

    a. What was in the tabernacle of the holy place? (9:2) (outer)

    b. What was behind the second veil? (9:3)

    c. What three things were in the Ark of the Covenant? (9:4)

        1.

        2.

        3.

    d. Where were the cherubim? (9:5)

    e. Who can enter the Holy of Holies? How often? Why? (9:7)

4. Read <u>Psalm 99</u>.

    a. Where is the LORD? (99:1)

    b. Who are we to worship? (99:5)

    c. Write what you learned about God. (99:8)

5. Read <u>Ezekiel 1:1-3</u>. What did Ezekiel see? (1:1)

6. Read <u>Ezekiel 9:3</u>. Where did the glory of the God of Israel go? (Same cherubim on mercy seat)

7. Read <u>Ezekiel 10:4</u>. What was the temple filled with?

8. Read <u>Ezekiel 10:18-19</u>.

   a. Where did the glory of God go to next? (10:18)

   b. Describe what happened when the cherubim departed. (10:19)

9. Read <u>Ezekiel 11:22-23</u>. Where did the glory of God go next?

10. Read <u>Zechariah 14:4</u> to find out the name of the mountain.

11. Read <u>Ezekiel 43:1-5</u>. Where did the glory of God come from? (43:2,4)

12. Read <u>Revelation 22:1-5</u>.

a. What is in the New Jerusalem that believers will someday eat from? (22:2)

b. Who will be there? (22:3)

c. Who will illumine them? (22:5)

FOCUS ON THE FACTS

Adam and Eve ate from the tree that God had forbidden them. God shed the first blood and made them garments of skin. They now knew good and evil and could no longer eat from the tree of life or live forever. God sent them out from the Garden of Eden and stationed the cherubim and the flaming sword which turned every direction to guard the way to the tree of life. The LORD spoke to Moses and the sons of Israel constructed the Ark of the Covenant covered with a pure gold mercy seat. One cherub at each end with their wings spread upward covered the mercy seat and faced one another. The ark contained the tables of the covenant (Ten Commandments), a jar of manna and Aaron's rod which budded. The tabernacle had an outer court called the holy place. The inner court was called the Holy of Holies. This contained the Ark of the Covenant where the cherubim of glory overshadowed the mercy seat. The high priest entered once a year, taking blood to atone for the sins of the people.

Ezekiel saw visions of God. The glory of God went up from the cherub to the threshold of the temple (filled with the cloud) and the court was filled with the brightness of the glory of the LORD. Then the glory of God stood over the cherubim. When they departed, they lifted their wings and rose up from the earth with the wheels beside them and stood still at the entrance of the east gate of the LORD's house and the glory of the God of Israel hovered over them. Then He (Jesus) stood on the Mt. of Olives. This will happen when Jesus returns. We will someday have a New Jerusalem (Heaven) where believers will eat from the tree of life and have everlasting life. We will be with God and Jesus and see Their face, serving Them.

SO WHAT?

Adam and Eve ate from the forbidden tree. **Genesis 2:17 but from the tree of the knowledge of good and evil you shall not eat, for in the day that you eat from it you shall surely die.** Adam and Eve did not listen and like them we are human and make mistakes. As believers we know what good and evil, right from wrong is and need to listen to God and obey Him. Read about the Ten Commandments in Exodus 20. Become a believer if you are not already. Our earthly bodies will die but as believers we will not go through a second death but be given eternal life. **John 3:16 For God so loved the world, that He gave His only begotten Son, that whoever believes in Him shall not perish, but have eternal life.**

We are to worship God because He answers prayer and forgives us. We no longer need to go to the Holy of Holies since Jesus became flesh and died for our sins. This is what John the Baptist said; **John 1:29 The next day he saw Jesus coming to him and said, "Behold, the Lamb of God who takes away the sin of the world!**

The cherubim are standing guard. We will be learning about cherubim with wheels next lesson.

Revelation 2:7 He who has an ear, let him hear what the Spirit says to the churches. To him who overcomes, I will grant to eat of the tree of life which is in the Paradise of God. Someday all believers will eat from the tree of life in heaven. If we don't meet in person, I will see you there.

CHERUBIM ARE STANDING GUARD

LORD'S PRAYER

LESSON THREE
Cherubim with Wheels

Share and care: What was your first car?
(year, make, model, color)

Prayer

1. Read <u>Ezekiel 1:4-21.</u>

   a. **What did Ezekiel see? (1:5)**

   b. **What did each living being have? (1:6)**

   c. **What was under their wings? (1:8)**

Cherubim from <u>Ezekiel 1:10.</u>

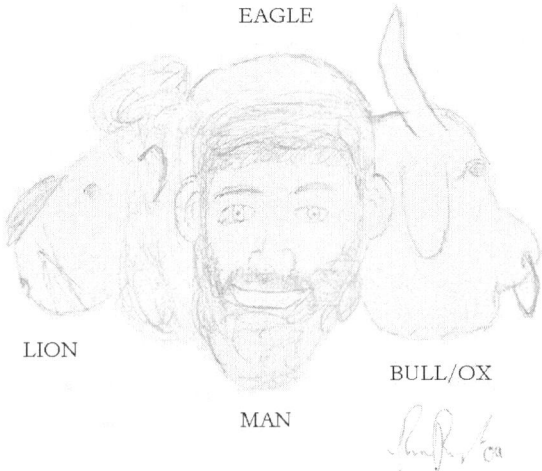

EAGLE

LION

BULL/OX

MAN

d. **What was seen in the midst of the living beings? (1:13)**

e. **What were they full of? (1:18)**

f. **What moved with the living beings? (1:19)**

g. **Where was the spirit of the living beings? (1:20-21)** (Under control of the spirit.)

2. **Read Ezekiel 1:22-28.**

a. **What was over the head of the living beings? (1:22)**

b. **How many wings did they have? (1:23)**

c. **What did the wings sound like? (1:24)**

d. **What happened to their wings when they heard a voice and stood still? (1:25)**

e. **What was seen over their heads? (1:26-28)**

3. Read <u>Ezekiel 10:1-3</u>.

    a. What are the living beings called? (10:1)

    b. What was the man clothed in linen to do? (10:2)

    c. Where were the cherubim? (10:3)

4. Read <u>Ezekiel 10:5-13</u>.
Verse 4 are different cherubim with no wheels.

    a. What did the sound of the wings of the cherubim sound like? (10:5)

    b. Who took fire and gave it to the one clothed in linen? (10:7)

    c. What did the cherubim's hands look like? (10:8)

    d. What did the wheels look like? (10:9)

    e. What were they full of? (10:12)

    f. What were the wheels called? (10:13)

5. Read <u>Ezekiel 10:14</u>. Draw the four faces below.

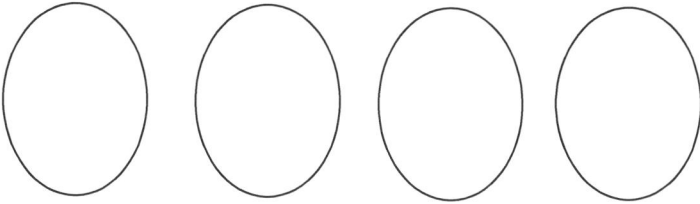

6. Read <u>Ezekiel 10:15-17</u>. What happened when the cherubim moved or stood still? What was in them?

7. Read <u>Ezekiel 10:20-22</u>. Where were the living beings? (10:20)

8. Read <u>Revelation 4:1-6.</u>

   a. What was John shown in heaven? (4:2)

   b. Who was around the throne? (4:4)

   c. What came out from the throne? (4:5)

   d. Who was in the center and around the throne? (4:6)

9. Read <u>Revelation 4:7</u>. Write out what each creature looked like.

    1.

    2.

    3.

    4.

10. Read <u>Revelation 4:8-11</u>.

    a. What did each of the creatures have? (4:8)

    b. What did they say day and night? (4:8)

    c. What do the living creatures give to Him who sits on the throne? (4:9)

    d. Who is worthy of this? Why? (4:11)

11. Share ways believers can give glory and honor and thanks to God and Jesus.

FOCUS ON THE FACTS

Ezekiel had a vision of four living beings (cherubim) that were in human form. They had four faces and four wings with human hands. Each had a face of a man, lion, bull and eagle. They would go where the spirit was about to go. Something like fire was in the midst of them. They each had a wheel where the spirit was. Their wings were the sound of abundant waters and the voice of the Almighty. They would drop their wings when still. Over their heads was a throne with the likeness of the glory of the LORD. The living beings are cherubim beneath the God of Israel. A cherub took fire from between the cherubim and gave it to the man clothed in linen. The cherubim were full of eyes all around with whirling wheels.

In Revelation, John was shown heaven with a throne that had 24 elders with crowns on thrones. In the center and around the throne were four living creatures (cherubim) like the ones Ezekiel described. They give glory, honor and thanks to Jesus and God who created all things.

SO WHAT?

Ezekiel was a prophet from Judah taken into exile by the Babylonians. He prophesied that God would keep His covenant. Imagine what abundant waters may sound like. I think the sound could have been like the falls in Yosemite National Park, CA.

God is on the throne and Jesus is at His right hand. **1 Kings 22:19 Micaiah said, "Therefore, hear the word of the LORD. I saw the LORD sitting on His throne, and all the host of heaven standing by Him on His right and on His left. Mark 16:19 So then, when the Lord Jesus had spoken to them, He was received up into heaven and sat down at the right**

hand of God. The cross reference of scripture for the seven Spirits of God in **Revelation 4:5** is from **Isaiah 11:2 The Spirit of the LORD will rest on Him, The spirit of wisdom and understanding, The spirit of counsel and strength, The spirit of knowledge and the fear of the LORD.** The faces in Revelation are very similar to those we learned about in Ezekiel. They say HOLY, HOLY, HOLY. As believers we should do the same! I use the New American Standard Bible (NASB) and when things are written in CAPITAL letters it means that it is also somewhere in the Old Testament. The verse in Revelation 4:8 is also found in Isaiah 6:3. Some believe that holy, holy, holy, refers to the trinity of God, Jesus and the Holy Spirit.

The meaning of Revelation 4:8 could be as follows; **WHO WAS,** Jesus was born a baby, He was made flesh (human) and died and rose again. **WHO IS,** Jesus is still alive and in heaven **WHO IS TO COME,** Jesus will come again to earth.

Doing this study about angels opens our eyes to what heaven is like and what cherubim really look like. The images we see of angels in our world may not truly represent what we have learned from the Bible to be true. Angels come in different forms which we will be learning more about. Share with others so the facts are correct.

CHERUBIM WORSHIP AND PRAISE GOD

LORD'S PRAYER

LESSON FOUR
Seraphim

Share and care: Where is your favorite vacation spot?

Prayer

Seraphim are celestial beings (angels) with six wings that purify. **Seraph** means "burning one".

1. Read <u>Isaiah 6:1-7.</u>

    a. Where did Isaiah see the LORD? (6:1)

    b. Describe the seraphim. (6:2)

    c. What were the seraphim saying? (6:3)
       (Similar to what Cherubim say in Rev 4:8)

    d. What filled the temple? (6:4)

    e. What was Isaiah confessing to? (6:5)

    f. How did the seraphim get to Isaiah? (6:6)

    g. What did the seraphim take from the altar? (6:6)

    h. What did the seraphim do with the burning coal? (6:7)

    i. Why was this done? (6:7)

2. Read <u>1 John 1:7</u>.

    a. How are we to walk?

    b. What will we have with one another?

    c. Who cleanses us from all sin?

3. Share ways that people are influenced to sin by those around them.

4. Why is it important to confess your sins before God?

5. Read <u>Isaiah 6:8-13</u>.

    a. Who did the work for the Lord and God (US)? (6:8) Notice the plural us was used showing both.

    b. If God asks you to do something how should you respond? (6:8)

    c. People's hearts were hardened but Isaiah did not give up. How many would return and go through a burning time? (6:13)

    d. What remained after the burning? (6:13)

6. Are there times when you have felt like you were burned but kept for God's purpose? Some may not want to share.

7. Read <u>Deuteronomy 7:6-13</u>.

    a. Why are a holy people chosen? (7:6)

    b. How many holy people are there? (7:7)

   c. What did the LORD do for the holy people? (7:8)

      1.

      2.

      3.

   d. Who is God talking about? (7:9)

   e. What happens to those who hate God? (7:10)

   f. What happens to those who love God? (7:11-13)

8. Do you think believers today are included? Why?

9. If comfortable, share an angel story with your group.

FOCUS ON THE FACTS

Isaiah was a prophet from Judah who was important to the kings. He prophesied what would happen to them and about the coming of Jesus. Isaiah saw the Lord sitting on a throne in a vision. Seraphim were above Him. They each used two wings to cover their face, two wings to cover their feet and two wings to fly. They were praising God. This is the only place in the Bible that seraphim are used. The seraphim were above the throne and had 6 wings. The cherubim were around the throne and had 4-6 wings. The temple was filled with smoke or the glory of the LORD. Isaiah thought he was ruined since he was a man of unclean lips and was influenced by those around him. The seraphim flew to him with a burning coal and touched his mouth so his sin would be taken away and forgiven. The seraphim were used for the cleansing but God is the one who cleanses believers from sin.

In the Old Testament, Jesus had not yet died for people's sins so they had to be forgiven with burnt offerings. Isaiah was willing to do God's work. Sometimes it seems that people's hearts are hardened and do not want to know about Jesus. Believers need to keep sharing the good news. After 70 years in Babylon a tenth returned and went through some hard times but Israel would survive from a stump (holy seed). The holy people were chosen for God's own possession even though only a few in number. God loves us and kept His oath that we would be redeemed from slavery. He is faithful to those who love Him and keep His commandments but will destroy those who hate Him.

SO WHAT?

Do you feel ruined by something that you have done? Do you think that you have an unforgiveable sin that cannot be taken away? We all sin but we are not to habitually sin the same thing over and over. Pray and ask Jesus to help you in the area you struggle with. It is important that you believe and ask Jesus for forgiveness. **Ephesians 1:7 In Him we have redemption through His blood, the forgiveness of our trespasses, according to the riches of His grace.** Do not be influenced by others around you that could potentially lead you to sin. Ask Jesus to help you stay clean. **Colossians 1:13-14 For He rescued us from the domain of darkness, and transferred us to the kingdom of His beloved Son, in whom we have redemption, the forgiveness of sins.** Walk in the light because Jesus is the Light.

The passage from Isaiah was meaningful to me. Many times while writing I have said, "Here I am, Lord help me!" Let God touch your lips and purify you from all your sin. Even if your life is a mess and you feel like you have been burned, you still have a stump that will remain that can grow again like new. My family and I travelled to Yellowstone National Park in WY. Our first trip was when the forest was lush and green. The other trip was after the devastating fire that destroyed much of the forest area. We were amazed by the re-growth that we could see coming up from the burned ground. Jesus can help re-grow your spirit at any time. He is the only one that can make you whole. Go to Him in prayer.

We all have to make a choice to love God and believe in Jesus or not. Our eternal life depends on this. It is never too late to change your life for the better. I am now writing this in the New Year 2009, after Christmas has just passed. Don't let the excitement of the birth of Jesus end but keep it going all year long.

SERAPHIM PURIFY AND PRAISE GOD

LORD'S PRAYER

LESSON FIVE
Angel Gabriel to Zacharias & Mary

Share and care: Why were you named? Was it after someone or parents liked it?

Prayer

1. Read <u>Luke 1:5-14</u>. The NIV uses Zechariah and NASB uses Zacharias.

   a. Who is the story about? (1:5)

   b. What kind of people were they? (1:6)

   c. Did they have children? (1:7)

   d. What was Zacharias to do? (1:8-9)

   e. Who appeared to Zacharias? Where? (1:11)

   f. How did it make Zacharias feel? (1:12)

   g. The angel told him not to be afraid. What message did he give? (1:13)

2. Read <u>Luke 1:15-17</u>. What did you learn about John?

    a. He will

    b. He will

    c. He will

    d. He will

    e. He will

3. Read <u>Luke 1:18-25</u>.

    a. What was Zacharias' question to the angel? (1:18)

    b. How often do we question what God tells us? Do we always get proof?

    c. Who was the angel? (1:19)

    d. Where does he stand? (1:19)

    e. Why was he sent? (1:19)

f. What would happen to Zacharias because of his unbelief? How long?(1:20)

g. Did what the angel say come true? (1:22-25)

4. Read <u>Luke 1:57-66</u>.

   a. What did Elizabeth want to name the baby? (1:60)

   b. What did Zacharias want to name the baby? (1:63)

   c. Where did they get the name from? (1:13,19)

   d. What happened after the baby was named? (1:64)

   e. What did the people think? (1:65-66)

5. How do you think you would react to seeing an angel?

6. Read <u>Luke 1:26-31</u>.

   a. After Elizabeth (in the 6th month); where was Gabriel sent? Who sent him? (1:26)

   b. Who was Gabriel to see? (1:27)

   c. What did you learn about her? (1:27)

   d. What did Gabriel tell Mary? (1:28)

   e. How did Mary react to Gabriel? (1:29)

   f. How did Gabriel reassure her? (1:30)

   g. What was to happen to Mary? (1:31)

7. Read <u>Luke 1:32-33</u>. What did you learn about Jesus?

   a. He will be

   b. He will be called

   c. He will be given

   d. He will reign over

   e. His kingdom will

8. Read <u>Luke 1:34-45.</u>

   a. What did Mary say to the angel? (1:34)

   b. What did the angel say to Mary? (1:35)

   c. What news did Mary learn about Elizabeth? (1:36)

9. Write out the verse from <u>Luke 1:37</u>. Memorize it.

10. **Share impossible things that God has done for you.** Not everyone will want to share.

11. **What was Mary's response? (1:38)** Then Gabriel departed from her.

12. **Where did Mary go? (1:39-40)**

13. **What happened to Elizabeth? (1:41)**

14. **What did she say about Mary? (1:42,45)**

   a. **Blessed are**

   b. **Blessed is**

   c. **Blessed is she**

15. **What did she know about Mary? (1:43)**

FOCUS ON THE FACTS

Zacharias and Elizabeth were righteous in the sight of God. They had no children. Zacharias was a priest and was chosen by lot to enter the temple of the Lord and burn incense. While there, an angel appeared and frightened him. The angel told him not to be afraid that they would have a son and name him John. He would be great to God, not drink wine or liquor, be filled with the Holy Spirit, turn many of Israel back to God and would be a forerunner before Jesus. Zacharias questioned the angel and wanted to know for certain that it would happen. The angel was Gabriel that stands in the presence of God and was sent to give the message about John. Because of Zacharias' unbelief he was made silent until John was born and named. What Gabriel said came true. John grew up and became known as John the Baptist who later baptized Jesus.

Gabriel was sent to Mary, a virgin who was engaged to Joseph and living in Nazareth. He told her that she had found favor with God and would conceive a Son by the Holy Spirit and that she should name him Jesus. Gabriel told Mary that He would be great, called the Son of the Most High and given the throne of His father David. He would also reign over the house of Jacob forever and His kingdom would have no end. Mary questioned the angel but was told that Elizabeth had also conceived and that nothing is impossible with God. Mary told Gabriel she was a bondservant of the Lord and may it be done according to his word. The angel departed and Mary hurried off to see if Elizabeth was pregnant. The baby leaped inside of Elizabeth and she was filled with the Holy Spirit. She knew that Mary was pregnant with the Lord. Mary believed that all the angel had said would come true.

SO WHAT?

Zacharias was from the priestly tribe and he would only be chosen to enter the temple once in his lifetime. How often do we question God when He gives us a message? Sometimes we get proof other times we do not. We have to have faith. We are NOT to put God to the test! Maybe there are times when we need to be silent and not speak. It is very difficult for me to keep quiet. Is this difficult for you too? I imagine the people were also wondering why Elizabeth and Zacharias would choose a name that was not a family name for their baby. They had fear and wondered what the child would turn out like. They knew the Lord was with him. Knowing what sex your baby is before they are born happens today since we have ultrasounds. Can you imagine if you knew about what your baby would do before it was born? How would that make you feel as a parent?

My class loved what the angel said to Mary, "Greetings, favored one! The Lord is with you," they thought it would be a great way to greet each other. What would happen if the ushers in church greeted people like this? As believers we are also favored. There was no current means of communication like phone or e-mail so Mary left in a hurry to see her relative Elizabeth to get proof. She trusted what the angel said but she wanted to verify that it was true. Know that God can do the impossible if it is in accordance to His will. He can do impossible things in your life too. When we become believers we are filled with the Holy Spirit. **John 14:26 But the Helper, the Holy Spirit, whom the Father will send in My name, He will teach you all things, and bring to your remembrance all that I said to you.**

You can read about the genealogy of Jesus in Luke 3:23-38. You can highlight some of the people that you may know in your Bible as shown below.

Lk 3:23 **Jesus** (born of the Virgin Mary by Holy Spirit) as was supposed, the son of **Joseph**, the son of **Eli** (through His mother, Mary)

Lk 3:31 …son of **David**

Lk 3:33…son of **Judah** (one of the 12 brothers)

Lk 3:34 the son of **Jacob**, the son of **Isaac**, the son of **Abraham**…

Lk 3:36… the son of **Shem**, the son of **Noah**…

Lk 3:38 the son of **Enosh**, the son of **Seth**, the son of **Adam**, the son of **God**.

GABRIEL GAVE MESSAGES

LORD'S PRAYER

PEOPLE THAT GOD NAMED IN THE BIBLE

Genesis 2:20 God named Adam
Genesis 3:20 Adam named Eve.

Genesis 16:11 Angel of the LORD told Hagar to name baby Ishmael
Genesis 17:5 God changed Abram's name to Abraham
Genesis 17:15 God changed Sarai's name to Sarah
Genesis 32:28, 35:10 God changed Jacob's name to Israel

Luke 1:13 Angel of the Lord told Zacharias to name his son John
Luke 1:31 Angel of the Lord told Mary to name her Son Jesus

John 10:1-18 Jesus calls His sheep by name and leads them out.
Luke 10:20 rejoice that your names are recorded in heaven. (In the Lamb's book of life)

LESSON SIX
Gabriel, Michael & Fallen Angels

Share and care: Think of a temptation that people face.

Prayer

1. Read <u>Daniel 8:15-19</u>.

   a. Who had a vision? (8:15)

   b. When he sought to understand the vision, who stood before him? (8:15)

   c. What did the voice say? Who was it? (8:16)

   d. What happened to Daniel when Gabriel came near? (8:17)

   e. What was the vision about? (8:17)

   f. What happened when Daniel fell into a deep sleep? (8:18)

   g. What did Gabriel want Daniel to know? (8:19)

2. Read <u>Daniel 9:20-23</u>.

    a. What was Daniel doing? (9:20)

       1.

       2.

       3.

    b. When did Gabriel appear? (9:21)

    c. Why did Gabriel appear? (9:22)

    d. What was Daniel to God? (9:23)

    e. What was Daniel to do with the message? (9:23)

       1.

       2.

3. Who was Daniel praying to? (Dan 9:20)
Do **NOT** pray to angels! Pray to God!

4. Read <u>Daniel 10:10-20.</u>

    a. **Who was withstanding Daniel for twenty-one days? (10:13)**
These are Satan's angels (demons).

    b. **Who came to help Daniel? (10:13)** He is God's archangel who protects the affairs of Israel.

    c. **What did the angel who came to give Daniel understanding, tell him? (10:14)**
(This Godly angel is not Michael.)

    d. **What happened to Daniel when he heard? (10:15)**

    e. **What did the angel do to help Daniel? (10:16)**

    f. **What did the angel look like? (10:16)**

    g. **How was Daniel strengthened? (10:17-19)**

    h. **Where did the angel go? (10:20)**

5. **Share times when you have felt strengthened and know that it was from God.** Not everyone will want to share.

6. **Read Daniel 10:21-11:1.**

   a. **Who stands firmly with the angel against the evil forces? (10:21)**

   b. **What did Michael do for Daniel? (11:1)**

7. **Read Daniel 12:1.**

   a. **Who is Michael?**

   b. **What was going to happen?** This will occur at the end of time when Jesus returns again. (Learn more by taking our Daniel Bible Study.)

8. **Read 1 Thessalonians 4:13-18. When the Lord descends from heaven who will announce Him? (4:16)** Jude 1:9 Michael.

9. Read <u>Jude 1:5-10</u>. (This is Jesus ½ brother.)

    a. What happened to the fallen angels in (1:6)

    b. What did the false teachers do? (1:8)

      1. Defile the

      2. Reject

      3. Revile

    c. Who was Michael? Who did he dispute with? (1:9)

    d. Who was Michael going to let rebuke? (1:9)

10. Read <u>Revelation 12:7-10</u>.

    a. Where did the dragon and his angels come from? (12:8)

    b. Who were they waging war against? (12:7)

    c. What does Satan do? (12:9,10)

      1. Deceives

      2. Accuses

    d. What happened to Satan and his angels? (12:9)

11. Read <u>Revelation 12:11-12</u>.

   a. How do believers overcome Satan and his angels? (12:11)

      1. The blood of

      2. Word of

      3. Do not love

   b. Who rejoices when the devil and his angels are thrown out of heaven? (12:12)

12. Read <u>Matthew 4:1-11</u>.

   a. Who tempted Jesus three times? (4:1)

   b. What should man live on? (4:4)

   c. Who could help Jesus? (4:6)

   d. What was Jesus' response? (4:7)

   e. Jesus told Satan to go, what did He say? (4:10)

   f. After the devil left Him, who came to minister to Him? (4:11)

FOCUS ON THE FACTS

Daniel wanted to understand a vision so He sent the angel Gabriel to give understanding. When the angel came near Daniel was frightened. He fell on his face and then into a deep sleep. Gabriel touched Daniel and made him stand upright. He told him about what would happen at the appointed time of the end. Gabriel came to Daniel a second time while he was speaking (aloud) and praying, confessing and presenting supplication before God both for himself and the people of Israel. He was not even finished when God heard and sent Gabriel to him. The angel came because Daniel was highly esteemed to God. Daniel was to give heed to the message.

Michael is the archangel from God who protects the affairs of Israel. There was another Godly angel that came to give Daniel understanding about what will happen in the future. Daniel was speechless. The angel was able to strengthen Daniel because God wanted him to and then he went back to fight against Satan's angels. Michael stands firmly against the evil forces. He was there to be an encouragement and protection for Daniel. Michael is the great prince who stands guard. There will come a time of distress and those whose names are found written in the book of life (believers) will be saved. Jesus will return, announced by Michael.

There are false teachers that defile the flesh, reject authority and revile angelic majesties. There are also fallen angels that are kept under darkness. Michael disputed with the devil but knew his place and let the Lord be the one to rebuke him. Michael and his angels waged war with the dragon (Satan) and his angels in heaven. The dragon and his angels were thrown down to earth. Those in heaven rejoiced. Satan deceives the whole world and is the accuser. Jesus was even tempted by the devil. We are to live on every word of God. Do not put God to the test. We are to worship and serve God only. God is with us and will help, sometimes He sends angels to minister to us like they did for Jesus.

SO WHAT?

Remember to pray to God for everything and not to angels. God is the one that can command an angel to give believers a message if He wants to. Angels can come and physically touch us if needed. Have you felt the touch of an angel? Daniel was speechless and we may have reacted the same way if we had gotten the news. We need to pray for others as well as ourselves and make our requests known. God can hear our prayers and answer them before we are even finished.

Do not remain speechless from what you know. God has given us the Bible so we will tell others about what will happen in the future. God is there protecting us and sometimes He uses angels. Believers have overcome Satan because Jesus died for our sins. We are to give our testimony (personal experience about what Jesus has done in your life) and be willing to even die for what we believe in. As Christians we are not to deny Jesus or fear death. As believers we want to go to heaven. Be strengthened and encouraged that believers will share a place in heaven with God, Jesus and His angels. We do not want the devil or his angels to lead us in the wrong direction. There is still an earthly battle being waged over people. There will be false teachers and we need to check what they say with Scripture so we know what is true. **Romans 12:21 Do not be overcome by evil, but overcome evil with good.**

**GABRIEL GIVES UNDERSTANDING
MICHAEL IS THE PROTECTOR
SATAN DECEIVES AND USES FALLEN ANGELS**

LORD'S PRAYER

LESSON SEVEN
Jesus & Angels

Share and care: What do you like about Christmas, besides Jesus' birth?

Prayer

1. Read <u>Matthew 1:18-25</u>.

   a. What did Joseph plan to do with Mary? (1:19)

   b. Who appeared to Joseph in a dream? (1:20)

   c. What was Joseph told? (1:20-21)
   Gabriel was sent to Mary.

   d. What did Joseph do? (1:24-25)

2. Read <u>Luke 2:7-20</u>.

   a. Who appeared to the shepherds? How did they react? (2:9)

   b. What did the angel tell them? (2:10-11)

c. What suddenly appeared? (2:13)

d. What were they doing? (2:13-14)

e. Where did the angels go? (2:15)

f. What did the shepherds do? (2:15-16,20)

3. Read <u>Matthew 2:13</u>. Who appeared to Joseph in a dream when the magi had gone? Why?

4. Read <u>Matthew 2:14-15</u>. What did Joseph do?

5. Read <u>Matthew 2:19-23</u>.

a. When did an angel of the Lord appear to Joseph in a dream again? (2:19)

b. Where did Joseph take Mary and Jesus? (2:20,22-23)

6. **Share a time when you depended on God when you moved to a new location.** Not all will answer.

7. **Read <u>John 12:20-33</u>.**

    a. **Where did the voice come from? (12:28-29)**

    b. **What did the voice say? Why? (12:28,30)**

8. **Read <u>Luke 22:39-46</u>.**

    a. **Where was Jesus? (22:39)**

    b. **What was He doing? (22:41-42)**

    c. **Who was sent to Him? What did he do? (22:43)**

9. **Read <u>Matthew 28:1-10</u>.**

    a. **Who came to look at Jesus' grave? (28:1)**

    b. **After the earthquake who appeared? What did he do? (28:2)**

   c. What did the angel tell the women? (28:5-7)

      1. Do not be

      2. He is not

      3. Go quickly and

10. Read <u>John 20:10-18</u>. Who did Mary see in the tomb? (20:12)

11. Read again <u>Exodus 25:17-22</u>. (from lesson 2)

   a. What was made for the mercy seat? Note how they were placed. (25:18-20)

   b. Who would meet there? (25:22)

12. Do you see the connection between the scripture from John and Exodus?

13. Read <u>Mark 16:9-20.</u> Where is Jesus now? (16:19)

14. Read <u>1 Peter 3:21-22</u>.

    a. Where is Jesus now? (3:22)

    b. Who did He go after? (3:22)

15. Read <u>Acts 1:6-11</u>.

    a. What do believers receive? (1:8)

    b. What are believers to do? (1:8)

    c. What happened to Jesus? (1:9)

    d. Who came while they were looking into the sky? (1:10)

    e. Where is Jesus now? (1:11)

    f. How will Jesus return? (1:11)

16. Read <u>1 Timothy 3:16</u>. Who was Jesus seen by?

17. Read <u>Hebrews 4:14-16</u>.

   a. Where has Jesus gone before us? (4:14)

   b. How can Jesus sympathize with us? (4:15)

   c. What do believers receive? (4:16)

18. Read <u>Hebrews 2:1-10</u>.

   a. What happened to the Son of Man (Jesus) for a little while? (2:7,9)

   b. Why was this done? (2:9)

FOCUS ON THE FACTS

Mary and Joseph were both given messages from angels that they would have a Son by the Holy Spirit and should call him Jesus. He would save His people from sins. While shepherds watched their flock by night, an angel told them about Jesus and suddenly a multitude of the heavenly host praised God. Magi followed a star to bring gifts to Jesus. After they had gone, an angel of the Lord appeared to Joseph in a dream and told him to flee to Egypt until the death of Herod. The angel appeared again and told them to go to Nazareth.

An angel spoke to glorify the name of God. When Jesus was in the Garden of Gethsemane on the Mount of Olives, He began to pray. He wanted everything to be God's will and not His own. An angel was sent to strengthen Him. After Jesus' death on the cross He was placed in a tomb. When Mary Magdalene and the other Mary went to see where Jesus' body was laid, an earthquake had occurred and an angel of the Lord had descended from heaven and rolled away the stone. He told them not to be afraid because Jesus was not there but had risen and to go tell His disciples. When Mary looked inside she saw two angels in white sitting one at the head and one at the feet where the body of Jesus had been lying. Jesus had risen and the angels were there. After appearing, He told His disciples to preach the gospel to all creation and wait for the Holy Spirit. Jesus ascended into a cloud to heaven having gone after angels and authorities and powers had been subjected to Him. He is seated at the right hand of God. Two men in white clothing told the men that Jesus will come back again in the same way, descending in a cloud. This is the 2nd coming of Christ. Jesus had come to earth as man and can sympathize with us. He had been tempted but did not sin. We may receive mercy and find grace to help us in our time of need.

Jesus was made flesh and blood as a human, lower than the angels for a little while. By the grace of God, Jesus tasted death for everyone. He died on the cross for our sins and is able to come to our aid when we are tempted. While on earth we are also lower than angels. We are to praise the name of Jesus and put our trust in Him not angels.

SO WHAT?

Married to an Air Force husband we moved many times and had to depend on God wherever we lived. You can depend on Him for everything. Joseph and Mary had no relations and she was with child by the Holy Spirit. Joseph would have to send her away since they were not yet married but wanted to do it secretly. Have times changed with unwed pregnancies today? Did you notice when angels appeared they usually said, "Do not be afraid." Joseph was told to marry Mary, she would have a Son and to name Him Jesus. They also got to know what the baby was before ultrasound. Imagine being told that your baby would save people from their sin. Joseph did what the angel said and took Mary as his wife. He kept her a virgin until the birth of Jesus. **Matthew 13:55-56** tells that Mary and Joseph had other children; James, Joseph, Simon, Judas (Jude) and sisters (more than one but not named). These siblings would be half brothers and sisters of Jesus. Joseph obeyed and left for Egypt until the death of Herod. This fulfilled the prophecy; out of Egypt, I called My Son from **Numbers 24:8.**

We can pray like Jesus did in the garden. Let God's will be done in your life not by your own will. He is the one that will give you strength. Did you remember that God met the people between the two cherubim on the mercy seat when you re-read Exodus? Angels were there throughout Jesus' life. God used them to give messages and to guard. Angels are still around today. If we are instructed to tell others a message we should go quickly and do it. Jesus is seated at the right hand of God. This made me think of the saying, "Your right hand man." Think of how important this is to have Jesus on your side. We receive power when the Holy Spirit comes upon us as believers. Missionaries are still sent out all over the world to be witnesses for Jesus. If he calls upon you, be ready to go and serve.

Jesus will one day return descending in a cloud and we need to be ready. Jesus had been tempted in all things as we are, yet without sin. We will be given a way out from sin when tempted. Can you think of an example of when this happened to you? I like to pray when I feel tempted for God to rescue me from my sin before I do it. If we sin we need to ask for forgiveness. Jesus tasted death for everyone. We do not need to be afraid to die because there is eternal life for believers.

ANGEL STRENGTHENED JESUS

LORD'S PRAYER

LESSON EIGHT
Amount of Angels and Purpose

Share and care: Name a large number. Describe something you could see with that amount. (ex. Myriads of angels.)

Prayer

1. Read <u>Matthew 18:1-6, 10-14</u>.

   a. After Jesus called a child to Himself, what did He tell the disciples to do?

      1. (18:3)

      2. (18:4)

      3. (18:5)

   b. Where are angels? (18:10)

   c. Who do they see? (18:10)

   d. What is the will of the Father in heaven? (18:14)

2. Read <u>John 1:51</u>. What are the angels doing?

3. Read <u>Genesis 28:10-17</u>. What did Jacob see in his dream? (28:12)

4. Read <u>Genesis 32:1-2</u>. Who met Jacob? What did he name the camp?

5. Read <u>2 Thessalonians 1:3-12</u>. Who will come with Jesus? (1:7)

6. Read <u>Jude 1:14-16</u>. Who did Enoch prophesy would come? Why? (1:14,15)

7. Read <u>Deuteronomy 33:1-2</u>. Where did Moses tell the people that God came from?

8. Read <u>1 Kings 22:19</u>. Who was with the LORD?

9. Read <u>Daniel 7:9-10</u>. How many angels are attending the Ancient of Days (God)?

10. Read <u>Revelation 5:11</u>. How many angels are around the throne?

11. Read <u>Hebrews 12:22</u>. How many angels are in the heavenly Jerusalem? The word means countless or innumerable.

12. Read <u>Matthew 26:51-54</u>. How many angels could God send to Jesus?

13. Read <u>Luke 2:13</u>. What did the shepherds see?

14. Read <u>Hebrews 1:6-14</u>.

   a. Who worships Jesus? (1:6)

   b. What are the angels like? (1:7)

   c. Jesus and God are forever and forever (and have not changed) who are they above? (1:9)

   d. What are the angels to do? (1:13,14)

15. Read <u>Psalm 91:11-12</u>. What are angels to do?

16. Read <u>Matthew 4:6-7</u>. What could God have done for Jesus? Jesus would not be tempted by the devil.

17. Read <u>Psalm 34:4-22</u>.

   a. What will the angel of the LORD do? (34:7)
   God can send angels to protect us.

   b. Who does the LORD redeem? (34:22)

FOCUS ON THE FACTS

Jesus called a child to Himself and told the disciples that they were to be converted and become like children. They were to humble themselves and receive others as children of God, not causing believers to stumble. God does not want anyone to perish. Angels can see the face of God in heaven. Angels can ascend and descend from heaven to earth. Jesus will return again with His mighty angels in flaming fire. The holy ones are many thousands and Jesus will execute judgment upon the ungodly. God is on His throne in heaven with thousands and thousands of angels attending Him and myriads upon myriads (uncountable number) standing before Him. God could have sent more than twelve legions (A Roman legion was between 3,000 and 6,000 so 12 legions could mean 72,000) of angels to Jesus at any time while He was on earth. An angel told the shepherds not to be afraid, because Jesus had been born. Suddenly a multitude of the heavenly host was praising God. What a sight that must have been.

The angels (like wind and fire) worship Jesus. He is above them. He made the heavens and the earth and has not changed but is the same forever. Angels are ministering spirits sent out from God to serve believers. They will guard us. God can send one angel, several or myriads of them. God will protect and rescue believers; someday He will redeem us for eternal life. God could have sent angels to rescue Jesus but Jesus died, was raised from the dead and will come again to fulfill Scripture.

SO WHAT?

While writing this from the second floor of our house (built in 1840), three bald eagles flew past the window. Their wings were huge and they flew gracefully. They proceeded to swoop around before landing upon our 100+ year old trees. Okay, I had to take a break to find the camera and get a photo. I kept looking and praising God for the beauty of the eagles. After a couple of photos they flew away. I can only imagine what it must have been like to see so many angels at one time praising God. I had not seen eagles here before. Did God send them? I know He did!

Hebrews 1:14 Are they not all ministering spirits, sent out to render service for the sake of those who will inherit salvation? Angels can be sent out to help believers today. They can encamp around us and rescue us. **Psalm 34:13-14. Keep your tongue from evil and your lips from speaking deceit. Depart from evil and do good; Seek peace and pursue it.**

ANGELS CAN ASCEND, DESCEND AND RESCUE

LORD'S PRAYER

Bald Eagle in Maquoketa, Iowa
January 2009

LESSON NINE
Angels Worship & Praise

Share and care: What is your favorite worship song?

Prayer

1. Read <u>Psalm 103:19-22</u>.

    a. Where is the LORD? (103:19)

    b. Who does His sovereignty rule? (103:19)

    c. Write what you learned about angels, hosts and servants. (103:20-21) Notice the cover title is from this scripture.

        1. Mighty in

        2. Perform

        3. Obey the

        4. Doing

    d. Where are those who bless the LORD? (103:22)

2. Do you think that people are acting as servants of the LORD? Why or Why not?

3. Read <u>Psalm 148:1-6</u>. Who are we to praise? Why? (148:5-6)

4. Read <u>Nehemiah 9:5-6</u>. Who praises and bows down before the LORD?

5. Read <u>Hebrews 1:6</u>. What do the angels do?

6. Read <u>Revelation 5:11-14</u>. Who gives blessing and honor and glory to God and Jesus? (5:13)

7. Read <u>Revelation 7:9-17</u>.

   a. Who was standing before the throne of God and Jesus? (7:9-10)

   b. What did the angels do? (7:11)

   c. Who are the ones clothed in white robes? (7:14)

   d. What happens to them? (7:15-17)

8. Read <u>Matthew 10:24-33</u>

    a. Why should believers fear God? (10:28)

    b. What should believers do? (10:32)

    c. What happens to unbelievers? (10:33)

9. Read <u>Isaiah 41:10</u>. Write out this verse and memorize it if you want to.

10. Read <u>Luke 15;1-10</u>.

    a. What can cause joy in heaven? (15:7)

    b. Who is rejoicing over one sinner who repents? (15:10)

11. Read <u>Colossians 2:18-19</u>. We are to hold fast to Christ and NOT worship who?

12. Read <u>Revelation 22:8-9</u>. When John fell down to worship the angel, what did he tell him?

13. Read <u>Revelation 19:10</u>. What is the testimony of Jesus? ´

14. Read <u>2 Timothy 4:1-5</u>. When should you be ready to preach the word? How? (4:2)

15. Read <u>Luke 4:10</u>. What can God command His angels to do?

FOCUS ON THE FACTS

God is on His throne in heaven and rules over all. Angels are mighty in strength, perform and obey His voice. (Notice the title of this study.) All His hosts and servants do His will. I believe that all of us are called to do God's work. We are to be His servants doing His will. Are you listening and obeying the voice of God? God wants you to be obedient. If there are things that need changing about your life then do it! Join the angels and heavenly host in worshiping and praising God and Jesus. There are a great multitude, angels, elders and the four living creatures that fall down and worship God and Jesus. Do you worship God? Have you confessed that you are a believer? Do not deny Jesus or you will be denied before God. Believers will have eternal life. God is able to destroy those who do not believe in Him. Both their soul and body will be in hell.

There is joy in heaven in the presence of the angels of God when one sinner repents. Have you caused the heavens to rejoice lately? Repenting of your sins can be done at any time. Be the one that causes rejoicing in heaven. Confess your sins and feel renewed by God. Do not worship angels but hold fast to Christ. Worship God! Angels are servants of God and can be sent to guard believers. We are to share the testimony of our faith about Jesus so others will know about Him. We are to be ready at anytime (in season or out) to share our faith stories and the Word of God. Reprove, rebuke, exhort (encourage) with great patience and instruction. Some people may not listen but do not give up. Write out your story and keep it in your Bible. Share it with your family and friends.

SO WHAT?

As I write this, the ground is a blanket of snow. It makes me think about changes that occur on the earth. There is a season for everything. Anytime is a great time for making a change to be more obedient to God's voice. God rules over all. People are not puppets and do have free will. Do you think that many of the bad things that happen in the world today are caused by people trying to do what they want and not obeying God? We are not perfect and sin but we are to live as servants of the LORD and be good examples for others as Christ was.

The Bible verse from **Isaiah 41:10** is special to me because I found it highlighted in my Grandma Irene Deppey's Bible. I have repeated it many times over the years, usually when I felt afraid. I would instantly feel calm and a sense of God and His angels near. I pray that you will feel them too. We are NOT to worship ourselves or angels. In our society it is tempting to think that we need to help ourselves and think that we are wonderful or superior but we need to remember that it is not all about ourselves but it should be all about God and helping others. Are you heeding the words of the Bible? Jesus is revealed to us as we study and know the Word of God. Remember to worship God not angels or anyone else.

ANGELS OBEY GOD'S VOICE, DO HIS WILL, PRAISE AND WORSHIP HIM.

LORD'S PRAYER

LESSON TEN
Angels with Messages

Share and care: What was your first pet or the one you had the longest?

Prayer

1. Read <u>Numbers 22:12-38.</u> BALAAM

   a. Moab was in fear of the sons of Israel. They wanted Balaam to curse the people so they could defeat them. What did God tell Balaam to do? (22:12)

   b. The leaders of Moab asked Balaam again to help them. What did Balaam know about God? (22:18)

   c. What were God's instructions to Balaam? (22:20)

   d. Balaam went without the men coming to him. Who did God send to stop Balaam? (22:22)

   e. Who did the donkey see? How many times did he stop him? (22:23-27)

    f. Who talked to Balaam? Why? (22:28)

    g. What did Balaam see when the LORD opened his eyes? (22:31)

    h. What did Balaam do in <u>Num 22:34</u>?

    i. The angel of the LORD told him to go. What was he to speak? (22:35,38)

2. Read <u>1 Kings 19:1-8</u>. ELIJAH

    a. Elijah wanted to die. The LORD sent an angel. What did he do two times? (19:5,7)

    b. What did Elijah eat? How long did it last? (19:6,8)

3. Read <u>2 Kings 6:15-23</u>. ELISHA

    a. A great army surrounded Elisha. Who did the LORD send to help? (6:17)

    b. What did God do to the people after Elisha prayed? (6:18,20,23)

4. Read <u>1 Chronicles 21:1-30</u>. DAVID

   a. What did God allow Satan to do? (21:1)

   b. What did David do? (21:8)

   c. Why was David in distress? (21:13)

   d. Who did God send to destroy Jerusalem? Was it destroyed? (21:15,14)

   e. What did the angel of the LORD say? (21:18)

   f. Did David listen to the angel? (21:26)

5. Read <u>Daniel 3:23-28</u>. SHADRACH, MESHACH & ABED-NEGO

   a. Who was the fourth man in the fire? (3:25)

   b. Who did God send? Why? (3:28)

6. Read <u>Daniel 6:19-23</u>. DANIEL

   a. Who did God send to help Daniel? (6:22)

   b. Why was Daniel not injured? (6:23)

7. Read <u>Acts 8:26-40</u>. PHILIP

   a. Who did the angel of the Lord speak to? Why? (8:26)

   b. Where did the Spirit tell Philip to go? (8:29)

   c. After Philip preached Jesus and baptized the eunuch what happened? (8:39)

8. Read <u>Acts 10:1-5</u>. CORNELIUS saw an angel of God and was alarmed. What did he say? (10:4-5)

9. Read <u>Acts 10:21-23</u>. Why did CORNELIUS send for Peter? (10:22)

10. Have you ever felt God (or one of His angels) leading you to give a message to someone?

11. Read <u>Acts 12:1-11</u>. PETER

    a. How did the angel appear to Peter? (12:7)

    b. What did the angel want Peter to do? (12:8)

    c. Where did Peter and the angel go? (12:9-10)

    d. What did Peter know for sure? (12:11)

12. Read <u>Acts 12:22-23</u>. What happened to HEROD? Why?

13. Read <u>Acts 27:21-26</u>. PAUL wanted the men to keep up their courage. Why? (27:23-25)

14. Read <u>Judges 6:11-24</u>. GIDEON

    a. Who did the angel of the LORD come to? (6:11)

    b. What did the angel say? (6:12)

c. What was Gideon told? (6:14,16)

d. Gideon made an offering to God. Who did he
see? (6:21-22)

FOCUS ON THE FACTS

The people of Moab wanted Balaam to curse the
sons of Israel. Balaam knew that he could not do
anything contrary to the command of God. How are you
doing? Do you follow the commands of God? God sent
an angel of the LORD to Balaam three times to stop him
that only the donkey could see. The donkey spoke to
Balaam and the LORD opened Balaam's eyes so he
could see the angel standing in the way. Balaam
repented and the LORD wanted him to continue speaking
only His word.

Elijah wanted to die and told the LORD to take his
life. The LORD sent an angel two times and told him to
arise, eat and drink. It gave him strength for forty days
and forty nights. Does God strengthen you?

Elisha was a prophet and helped the king of Israel.
The king of Aram (Syria) was enraged. He went out with
a great army. When Elisha prayed to God, He sent
horses and chariots of fire to help him. After blinding the
Arameans and returning their sight he gave them a feast.
This showed the power of God and they did not come
again.

Satan took a stand against Israel. David was
moved to take a census of Israel. God was displeased
and struck Israel. David told God he had sinned greatly
and wanted to be forgiven. God sent an angel to destroy
Jerusalem. David saw the angel with his sword and fell
on his face. The angel told Gad to tell David to build an

altar to the LORD which he did. He offered burnt and peace offerings. The angel put his sword back into its sheath.

God sent an angel to a fiery furnace to rescue the men who served, trusted and worshiped no other gods. He sent an angel to shut the mouths of lions because Daniel served and trusted God.

Philip listened to the angel of the Lord and preached Jesus to the eunuch and baptized him. He was then snatched away to continue preaching the gospel.

Cornelius saw an angel of God in a vision and was divinely directed by him to send for Peter and hear a message. Sometimes God uses his angels to get messages to other people.

Peter was in prison awaiting death. The Lord sent forth His angel to rescue him. Peter's chains fell off and he followed the angel out of prison past two guards and a gate and then the angel departed. Peter knew for sure that the Lord had sent the angel. Have you ever been rescued?

Herod did not give God the glory and an angel of the Lord struck him and he was eaten by worms and died.

Paul had seen an angel of God that told him not to be afraid. He encouraged the men on his ship to believe that God would protect them as He said. Do you believe in God? He will protect you if you glorify (honor) Him.

Gideon was from a family that was considered the least in Manasseh and he was the youngest in his father's house. An angel of the LORD appeared to him and told him the LORD was with him. He was to deliver Israel from the hand of Midian. Gideon made an offering and the angel of the LORD appeared to put fire on the meat and bread and then vanished. The LORD told him that he would not die.

SO WHAT?

Are you as stubborn as a mule? Is it hard to admit your sin before God? We need to repent from our sins. God wants us to obey Him and speak His words. By taking Bible studies you learn the word of God so you can speak His words. We have the freedom of choice and try to do things on our own. Doing things with God is much easier than being alone. Pray to God to help you in all that you do. Let Him be a part of your decision making so it becomes His will and not your own or He may send an angel to get in your way. Sometimes we just need to open our eyes so we can see danger. Do you think your animals ever helped to rescue you from harm?

The horses and chariots of fire were angels. These could have been the cherubim with wheels that we learned about in lesson three. We are to listen to God and not Satan or his fallen angels. Sometimes there are consequences for your sins that affect others so think before you act. Can you think of examples?

Are you serving and trusting God? Do you think God can rescue you from harm? Sometimes our physical bodies are saved and other times we are saved and redeemed for eternal life and go to heaven.

Have you been told to call or visit someone that needed a message from God? Be listening, God can use you to share some news. I have felt God leading me to write these Bible studies and share with others. I give God the glory for what He has done. Many times God used ordinary people to accomplish what He wanted done. Be open to what God is calling you to do.

ANGELS CAN BE INVISIBLE, VISIBLE, ONE OR MORE. THEY CAN GUARD, HELP FIGHT BATTLES AND GIVE MESSAGES.

LORD'S PRAYER

LESSON ELEVEN
Zechariah's Visions & Jesus' Return

Share and care: Have you ridden a horse?

Prayer

1. Read <u>Zechariah 1:7-21</u>. He had visions.

   a. Who did the word of the LORD come to? (1:7)

   b. Who did God send to give the message? (1:9)

   c. How did the LORD speak to the angel? (1:13)

2. Read <u>Zechariah 2:1-5</u>. Future Jerusalem was measured. Who would be a wall of fire around and would be in her? (2:5)

3. Read <u>Zechariah 3:1-10</u>.

   a. Who was with Joshua in the vision? (3:1)

   b. Joshua would be cleansed from sin. What did the angel tell him to do? (3:7)

4. Read <u>Zechariah 4:1-14</u>. Who did the angel say the two olive branches were? (4:14)

5. Read <u>Zechariah 6:1-8</u>.

    a. Describe the horses and where they went.

       1st chariot (6:2)

       2nd chariot (6:2,6)

       3rd chariot (6:3,6)

       4th chariot (6:3,6)

    b. What did the angel say the chariots were? (6:5,7-8)

6. Read <u>Revelation 7:1-4</u>. John saw four angels. What were they doing? (7:1)

7. Read <u>Matthew 24:23-39</u>.

    a. Who will mislead people about Christ's return? (24:24)

    b. How will Jesus return? (24:30)

    c. Who will Jesus send forth? (24:31)

    d. Who knows when Jesus will return? (24:36)

8. Read <u>1 Thessalonians 5:2-6</u>. How will the day of the Lord come? (5:2)

9. Read <u>1 Thessalonians 4:13-18</u>.

   a. Who do believers need to believe in? (4:14)

   b. How does the Lord return? (4:16)

   c. Who will go with the Lord? (4:14,17)

10. Read <u>Mark 8:38</u>. Do not be ashamed of Jesus. How will He come?

11. Read <u>2 Corinthians 11:14-15</u>. What does Satan and his angels (servants) do?

12. Read <u>1 Peter 5:8</u>. The devil prowls around like a roaring lion. What should we do?

13. Read <u>Matthew 25:41</u>. What will happen to the devil and his angels?

14. Read <u>Revelation 20:10-15</u>. Who is in the lake of fire? (20:10,14-15)

15. Read <u>Luke 20:27-38</u>. What did Jesus tell the Sadducees about marriage and death in the resurrection? (12:35-36)

FOCUS ON THE FACTS

Zechariah was a prophet that God used. He sent an angel to give him meaning to his visions while he was awake. God spoke to the angel with gracious and comforting words. Future Jerusalem was measured. God would be a wall of fire around her and the glory in her. Joshua was seen in a vision with an angel of the LORD and Satan trying to accuse him. Angels removed his filthy garments took his iniquity away and returned him to the priesthood. Joshua was to walk in the LORD'S ways and perform His service. He would gain free access to God and His angels. Zechariah also had a vision of a golden lampstand and two olive trees. The angel told him that they are two anointed ones who are standing by the Lord of the whole earth. Zechariah had a vision with four chariots. They each had different colored horses, red, black, white and dappled. The angel told him they are the four spirits of heaven going forth after standing before the Lord to patrol the earth. In Revelation John saw four angels holding back the four winds of the earth referring to those that Zechariah saw.

Jesus warns us not to be misled by false Christs and false prophets that will show great signs and wonders. Jesus will return on the clouds of the sky and will send forth His angels with a great trumpet and gather together His elect. (Look at the photo on the front of this study.) Jesus and the angels of heaven do not know when He will return but only God alone knows. The day of the Lord will come like a thief in the night and we are to be alert, sons of light and day. We need to believe that Jesus died and rose again to go with Him to heaven. Those who are asleep in Jesus and believers who are alive will meet the Lord in the air. Believers will be comforted by these words and unbelievers will mourn when the day comes. Satan and his angels with unbelievers (name not in book of life) will be thrown in the lake of fire. Once believers are taken to heaven they will no longer marry or die. They will have eternal life.

SO WHAT?

The Jewish people returned to Palestine after their captivity from Babylon in 538 B.C. Zechariah encouraged the people to rebuild the Temple in Jerusalem. (516 B.C.) Jerusalem was later destroyed in 70 A.D. The Wailing Wall is still standing.

Changing of the garments signified the cleansing and would also show future cleansing that would be done when Christ returned. We need to get rid of the old and be forgiven, accepting the new way of Jesus. The two anointed ones could be Joshua and Zerubbabel sons of oil? In **Revelation 11:3 And I will grant authority to my two witnesses, and they will prophesy for twelve hundred and sixty days, clothes in sackcloth.** These could be Elijah and Moses that prophesy 3 ½ years.

Babylon was the land of the North which was devastated by the Persians. During the end times Babylon will be destroyed. **Revelation 18:21 Then a strong angel took up a stone like a great millstone and threw it into the sea, saying, "So will Babylon, the great city, be thrown down with violence, and will not be found any longer.**

There are many people who pretend to know when the end times will occur but do not listen to them. Satan and his angels disguise themselves as angels of light and servants of righteousness. They prowl around like lions. Be on the alert! The Bible tells us the truth. God is the only one that knows when Jesus will return. Do not be deceived into believing what others say about when Jesus will return or about the end times. Believers need to stand firm in their faith. During the days of Noah people were not prepared and a flood destroyed them. Christ will come again and some will not be ready. Are there people today that predict the future? What are your thoughts about this? Remember what the Bible says.

ANGELS WITH TRUMPETS WILL BE SENT FORTH IN THE END TIMES BUT ONLY GOD KNOWS WHEN.

LORD'S PRAYER

LESSON TWELVE
Angels of Revelation

Share and care: Do you or would you like to play an instrument?

Prayer

1. Read <u>Revelation 1:1</u>. Who showed John the things which must soon take place?

2. Read <u>Revelation 1:3</u>. Blessed is he who...for the time is near.

    a.

    b.

    c.

3. Read <u>Revelation 3:5-6</u>. Believers will be found in the book of life. What happens to overcomers?

    a.

    b.

    c.

4. Read <u>Matthew 13:36-43</u>.

    a. Jesus saved the good seed. Who are they? (13:38)

b. Who are the tares (unbelievers)? Who sowed them?(13:38-39)

c. What is the harvest? (13:39)

d. Who are the reapers? (13:39)

e. What happens to the tares (unbelievers) at the end of the age? (13:40,42)

f. What happens to the righteous (believers)? (13:43)

5. Read <u>Revelation 5:1-7</u>.

a. God had a book with seven seals. What did the angel ask? (5:2)

b. John was told to stop weeping. Who was worthy to open the book? (5:5)

6. Read <u>Revelation 7:1-4</u>. What did the angel tell the four angels NOT to do? (7:3-4)

7. Read <u>John 6:26-29</u>. How do believers become sealed? (6:29)

8. Read <u>Revelation 8</u>.

   a. What did God give the seven angels? (8:2)

   b. What went up before God out of the angel's hand? (8:3-4)

   c. The angel threw fire of the altar to the earth. What followed? (8:5)

9. Write what happens when the angels sound the first four trumpets.

   1st (8:7) (land)

   2nd (8:8-9) (sea)

   3rd (8:10-11) (waters)

   4th (8:12) (sky)

10. Read <u>Revelation 9:1-4,10</u>. What happens when the 5th angel sounds the trumpet?

11. Read <u>Revelation 9:14-18</u>. What happens when the 6th angel sounds the trumpet? People did not repent.

12. Read <u>Revelation 10:7</u>. What happens in the days when the 7th angel is about to sound?

13. Read <u>Revelation 11:15</u>. What happens when the 7th angel's trumpet sounds? Who will reign forever and ever?

14. Read <u>Revelation 14:6-7</u>. What was the 1st angel doing? Who is the eternal gospel for?

15. Read <u>Matthew 24:14</u>. What will happen before the end will come?

16. **Read** <u>**Revelation 14:9-11**</u> **and write out what the 3rd angel says.** Think about the lake of fire. In <u>Revelation 14,</u> seven angels will reap the earth.

17. **Read** <u>**Revelation 15:5-8**</u>.

    a. **What did the seven angels have? (15:6,7)**

    b. **Where did they come from? (15:5)**

    c. **What did they look like? (15:6)**

18. **Read** <u>**Revelation 16.**</u> **Write what each bowl causes and to whom?** There are seven seals from <u>6:1-8:5</u> and seven trumpets from <u>8:6-9:21, 11:15</u>. The seven bowls are from <u>15:1-16:21</u>. They are different judgments following after each other with the wrath increasing.

1st bowl (16:2) (on earth)

2nd bowl (16:3) (into sea)

3rd bowl (16:4-7) (rivers, waters)

4th bowl (16:8-9) (the sun) **What did the men NOT do?**

5th bowl (16:10-11) (on throne) They had sores from the 1st bowl. **What did the men NOT do?**

6th bowl (16:12) (on great river Euphrates)

7th bowl (16:17-21) (upon the air and earth)

19. **What did the loud voice say? (16:17)** The wrath of God is finished.

20. **Read** <u>Revelation 19:17-18</u>. **An angel told the birds in midheaven to come for what? Who will this be done to?**

21. Read <u>Revelation 20:1-3</u>. What did the angel do with the great chain?

22. Read <u>Revelation 21:9-12</u>. What did the angel show John? Where were the angels?

23. Read <u>Revelation 22:1-7</u>. God sent an angel to John to show His bondservants what will happen. What are believers to do? (22:7)

FOCUS ON THE FACTS

An angel came to John (he had visions while on the island of Patmos) from Jesus to show him the things that would take place in the future. We are to read, hear and heed what is written in Revelation. Believers are the good seed, written in the book of life with our names confessed to God and His angels. Unbelievers are the tares, sons of the evil one who is the devil. There will be a harvest at the end of the age and the reapers are angels who will gather and burn with fire the unbelievers. Hear what is being said. Believers will be in the kingdom of God.

God who sits on the throne had a book with seven seals. An angel wanted to know who was worthy to open the book and break its seals. John was told that Jesus is worthy. Horses came from the first four seals. An angel told four angels not to harm the earth, sea or trees until the bondservants of God were sealed on their foreheads. Believers are sealed!

God gave seven angels trumpets. Another angel held a golden censer with incense and prayers of all the saints that went up before God. The angel's trumpets were sounded and a third of the earth was destroyed including land, sea and sky. A third of mankind was tormented by creatures but only those that did not have the seal of God on their foreheads. A third of mankind was killed by armies of horsemen. Those that were not killed would not repent. When the seventh trumpet is sounded then the mystery of God is finished. The kingdom of the world has become the kingdom of our Lord and of His Christ and will reign forever and ever. Before the end will come, the gospel will be preached to the whole world. There will come a time when angels will reap the earth and blood will be shed.

The last seven angels had golden bowls filled with the wrath of God that they poured on the people who had the mark of the beast. There will be painful sores, blood in the waters and the sun will scorch men and probably the earth. The world will be darkened and the Euphrates River will dry up so the kings from the east can gather for the war of the great day of God. The sky and earth will all be affected and the great city will fall. Finally, the wrath will be done. Many people will not repent but curse God. An angel will tell the birds to come for the great supper of God. An angel will also bound Satan with a chain for a thousand years and throw him into the abyss.

An angel showed John the holy city, Jerusalem coming down out of heaven from God. Twelve angels were at the twelve gates. Believers are to heed the words of Revelation.

SO WHAT?

Jesus is the lion from the tribe of Judah, the Root of David. **Matthew 2:6 AND YOU, BETHLEHEM, LAND OF JUDAH, ARE BY NO MEANS LEAST AMONG THE LEADERS OF JUDAH; FOR OUT OF YOU SHALL COME FORTH A RULER WHO WILL SHEPHERD MY PEOPLE ISRAEL.** Believers are sealed. How does this make you feel?

The end times are near but there are still those who need to hear about Jesus. Do you think the Gospel is being spread today? How is this done? As believers we are not to be afraid of what will happen in the end times but testify to others our faith stories. **Revelation 13:18 Here is wisdom. Let him who has understanding calculate the number of the beast, for the number is that of a man; and his number is six hundred and sixty-six.** The beast (antichrist) and false prophet (which causes people to worship the beast) will eventually end up in the lake of fire with Satan.

John 10:27-29 My sheep hear My voice, and I know them, and they follow Me; and I give eternal life to them, and they will never perish; and no one will snatch them out of My hand. My Father, who has given them to Me, is greater than all; and no one is able to snatch them out of the Father's hand. Jesus gives comfort to believers that they will have eternal life. If you are comfortable, share your faith stories with the group or anyone that God might be given you a nudge to share with. Tell the truth about angels and spread the word of God to others.

ANGELS WILL REAP THE EARTH.

LORD'S PRAYER

ABOUT ANGELS

1. Created for God.

2. Cherubim are standing guard.

3. Cherubim worship and praise God.

4. Seraphim purify and praise God.

5. Gabriel gave messages.

6. Gabriel gives understanding. Michael is the protector. Satan deceives and uses fallen angels.

7. Angel strengthened Jesus.

8. Angels can ascend, descend and rescue.

9. Angels obey God's voice, do His will, praise and worship Him.

10. Angels can be invisible, visible, one or more. They can guard, help fight battles and give messages.

11. Angels with trumpets will be sent forth in the end times but only God knows when.

12. Angels will reap the earth.

Psalm 103:20 **Bless the LORD, you His angels, Mighty in strength, who perform His word, Obeying the voice of His word!**
1 Thessalonians 4:16 **For the Lord Himself will descend from heaven with a shout, with the voice of the archangel and with the trumpet of God and the dead in Christ will rise first.**

Questions and answers printed by permission from www.gotquestions.org

Question: "Where did Old Testament believers go when they died?"

Answer: The Old Testament teaches life after death, and that all people went to a place of conscious existence called Sheol. The wicked were there (Psalm 9:17; 31:17; 49:14; Isaiah 5:14), and so were the righteous (Genesis 37:35; Job 14:13; Psalm 6:5; 16:10; 88:3; Isaiah 38:10).

The New Testament equivalent of Sheol is Hades. Prior to Christ's resurrection, Luke 16:19-31 shows Hades to be divided into two realms: a place of comfort where Lazarus was and a place of torment where the rich man was. The word hell in verse 23 is not "Gehenna" (place of eternal torment) but "Hades" (place of the dead). Lazarus's place of comfort is elsewhere called Paradise (Luke 23:43). Between these two districts of Hades is "a great gulf fixed" (Luke 16:26).

Jesus is described as having descended into Hades after His death (Acts 2:27, 31; cf. Ephesians 4:9). At the resurrection of Jesus Christ, it seems that the believers in Hades (i.e., the occupants of Paradise) were moved to another location. Now, Paradise is above rather than below(2 Corinthians 12:2-4).

Today, when a believer dies, he is "present with the Lord" (2 Corinthians 5:6-9). When an unbeliever dies, he follows the Old Testament unbelievers to Hades. At the final judgment, Hades will be emptied before the Great White Throne, where its occupants will be judged prior to entering the lake of fire (Revelation 20:13-15).

What Happens When We Die?

OLD TESTAMENT (BEFORE JESUS' BIRTH)	
SHEOL (Hebrew) Place of the dead divided into two areas	
Wicked People	**Paradise or Abraham's bosom** **Righteous people**

NEW TESTAMENT (BEFORE JESUS' DEATH)	
HADES(Greek) Place of the dead divided into two areas	
Place of torment	**Paradise** Place of comfort

NEW TESTAMENT (JESUS DIES)	
HADES(Greek) Place of the dead divided into two areas	
Place of torment	**Paradise** Place of comfort
	JESUS dies and descends here **JESUS resurrected and ascended to heaven taking the righteous to Paradise/Heaven**

NEW TESTAMENT (JESUS ASCENDED)	
HADES Place of torment (below)	**PARADISE** Place of comfort (which is now above)
UNBELIEVERS Not in book of life	**BELIEVERS** Name written in book of life
JUDGMENT Great white throne lake of fire (HELL)	**JUDGMENT** Heaven/New Jerusalem
ETERNAL PUNISHMENT	**ETERNAL LIFE**

TREE OF LIFE BIBLE STUDIES

DANIEL
Prophecy for God's Everlasting Kingdom

REVELATION
Hear and Heed the Words of Prophecy

SPIRITUAL GIFTS
Building up the Body of Christ

GALATIANS
Boast in the Cross

OLD TESTAMENT
Rooted in History

NEW TESTAMENT
Jesus Died Once for All

LENTEN CROSS
Transformation

GENESIS
Go Forth From Home

EXODUS
Slavery to Sanctuary

EPHESIANS
Sword of the Spirit is the Word of God

LUKE
Jesus Saves the Lost

****

ORDERS & FUTURE STUDIES
www.treeoflifebiblestudies.com